I0075053

THE LEMMING TRADER

KOON LIP CHOO

FOREXASIA
ACADEMY

FOREX ASIA ACADEMY

Copyright © 2010 by Koon Lip Choo.

All rights reserved
Published by Forex Asia Academy
www.ForexAsiaAcademy.com

No part of this publication may be reproduced, stored in a retrieval system, or transmitted, in any form or by any means, electronic, mechanical, photocopying, recording, or otherwise, without prior written permission of the publisher and author.

DISCLAIMER AND TERMS OF USE
This report contains the ideas and opinions of the author. The information contained in this report is strictly for educational purposes only. If you wish to apply the ideas contained in this report, you are taking full responsibility for your actions.

The author disclaims any warranties (express or implied), merchantability, or fitness for any particular purpose. The author shall in no event be held liable to any party for any direct, indirect, punitive, special, incidental, or consequential damages arising directly or indirectly from the use of any of this material, which is provided "as is", and without warranties.

ISBN: 978-981-08-6248-0

This book is available for special discounts for bulk purchases for sales promotions or premiums. Special editions, including personalized covers, excerpts of existing books, and corporate imprints, can be created in large quantities for special needs. For more information, write to Lemming@ForexAsiaAcademy.com.

Printed in the United States of America
Charleston, South Carolina

The Lemming Effect

A phenomenon where people, like lemmings that are rumoured to commit mass suicide, follow the crowd and listen to popular opinion with often fatal consequences in trading and investing.

THE
LEMMING TRADER

Contents

Preface

Welcome to The Lemming Trader, a first in trading psychology books that introduces us to the suicidal behaviour of lemming traders.

My name is Koon Lip, and I have been trading for more than 8 years. I have traded through many different modern market conditions and have seen first hand what such conditions can do to individual trading portfolios.

Let me start from the beginning. I want to build a foundation so that you can understand and know that I am no different than you are. Some of you may be more experienced and wiser than I am, but I know one thing with which you cannot disagree: There is no reason for you to make the same mistakes I did, and if you have already made those same mistakes, I hope that you can learn from the solutions that I have found.

I personally come from a middle-income family in Singapore. Since young, I have always wanted to have things that I don't have. I started small businesses since the age of 17 and hence I do have this go-do-it attitude towards entrepreneurship.

And you know what? In my university days, I majored in Applied Mathematics and minored in Technopreneurship. In the world of financial numbers, everything seems to be greener on the other side and I started trading since 21. The first 2 weeks have been good, but soon after, I paid my tuition fees to the market. The 'green' became so much redder. The good news is I was able to avoid filing for any type of bankruptcy. I simply faced adversity: I was overcome, but I overcame it and adapted.

The rest is history. In this book, I have put together what I feel to be an easy-to read analogy of how most traders behave like lemmings. The Lemming Trader lets you understand from the fatal mistakes of lemming traders so you don't find yourself drowning in the harsh, cold sea of the financial markets.

Acknowledgements

It was my 26th Birthday that I start conceptualizing a book. Like every author around, I want the book to be different, to stand up off the bookshelf and hopefully to give readers a new perspective through the contents. Over here, I would like to try to thank everyone that has been involved in this book without forgetting anyone.

Thank you my illustrator and concept designer Joey for making this book possible in the first place.

While the book was completed in late-2009, I hesitated to publish it. I wonder if this book will be accepted by the market. I decided to press on and I first presented this idea of Lemming Trader over a few powerpoint slides to my students and event participants. It's through the overwhelming response that gave me more confidence to launch this book.

Thank you for my people in Forex Asia Academy especially to Chee Seng, Ong Bak Yam and Mei Chen. Thank you my good friend KS Low, my good friend in strategizing our business and investment portfolios. Thank you my students who have wrote to me and let me understand more about how people react differently in trading. And the people I have worked with since the inception of Forex Asia Academy. It's through the experiences of working and trading together that crystallize the essences in this book.

Thank you my teachers and mentors in my life. Thank you my trading pals and friends in the Forex and trading community.

Thank you to my wifey Lowie for always been there for me, pushing me to complete this book and supporting me to achieve greater heights in my life journey. Life's full of ups and downs, and she has been a pillar to the volatility of my life.

Thank you to my dearest parents for raising me from birth, providing what they can and grooming me to where I am. My younger brother Koon Po (a truly brilliant scholar and banker) for inspiring me to be at least on par with his achievements...

And lastly, the capital market. It's through the cold-blooded nature of the market reality that propels me to keep moving positively and changing relentlessly, to be a better market player.

Thank you all!

~ this is
gob.

Lemmings are rodents that are notoriously rumoured to commit mass suicide when they migrate. While this may be but a myth, their association with this unusual behaviour has become used to refer to those who listen to popular opinion with often fatal consequences.

This book will introduce you to their lesser-known but not less common kind:

The Lemming Trader

INTRODUCTION

The Fatal Lemming Journey

Phase 1: Biting More than You can Handle

With teeth that don't ever stop growing, Gob is tempted to bite on more than he can chew. Find out how overconfidence, egoism and other lethal trading flaws you display can prevent your profits from soaring.

Phase 2: Herd Mentality

Living in a community means lemming Gob is prone to falling prey to mass opinion. Here, you'll learn to develop the right frame of mind to cut through market clutter and stay true to your plan.

Phase 3: The Plunge

Mysterious, powerful and unexplainable forces (I believe the humans call it fear and greed) make the lemming jump into the sea. Luckily for us, these powerful forces can be overcome through simple secrets revealed here.

Phase 4: The Regretful Realisation

Prevention is always better than cure. Before it's too late, avoid drowning in the sea of financial markets by having a sound trading system tailored for your needs. A free trader personality test and more can be found here.

Biting off more than gob
can handle

PHASE I

Biting More than You Can Handle

Like other rodents, the incisors (or teeth, for the uninitiated) of lemmings grow continuously, allowing them to bite on more than they can handle.

The lemming trader is no different. Initially, he follows his trading plan faithfully. But soon, as he sees traces of success, his confidence, greed and ambition grow bigger and bigger. They begin to get the better of him, and he is ready to gnaw at any tree he sees, before he is ready for bigger stakes.

Indeed, overconfidence, perfectionism and egoism are no strangers to any trader. The lemming trader gets frustrated and desperate. He gets figety and loses all good sense. Before long, he finds himself open to external influences.

The first chapter *The 3 Cardinal Sins of Trading* will uncover the deadliest vices of traders in detail and guide you towards overcoming them.

The 3 Cardinal Sins of Trading

To invest wisely, it is necessary to become aware of
all the temptations to behave foolishly.
Anonymous

Cardinal Sin 1: Overconfidence

Here's something interesting to chew on: Studies regarding behavioural finance have found that three quarters of all traders rate themselves as 'above average', when it is obvious that only half of all traders can be better than the other half.

This overconfidence is what affects our actual trading performance. But before we condemn overconfidence, one must realise that there would be little trading in financial markets without it. The trick is to let the overconfidence of other lemming traders benefit you, while keeping your own confidence in check.

Having lost sight of potential risks, lemming traders may place themselves in bad trades as they do not realise that they are at an informational disadvantage.

Losses follow those who do not respect the market. Without sufficient appreciation of the market complexity and trading challenges, overconfident traders set very narrow confidence bands with low high guesses and high low guesses. A couple of others may think that by purchasing the latest softwares and sharpening their teeth, they're ready to take on any market.

Overconfident traders tend to overtrade, resulting in the massive trading volume we see in markets. In studies where traders were shown randomly generated price patterns and asked to indicate their confidence in predicting the market direction, the traders with the highest confidence in their predictions traded most frequently and suffered the greatest losses.

Overconfident traders do not believe in learning curves. Instead of starting small and slowly building up their portfolio, they want huge profits immediately. Unfortunately, their overconfidence makes them believe the latter is possible, and they jump recklessly into trades without clear understanding of the market.

And then there are the overconfident beginners who use a high level of leverage, hoping to get rich fast. Those who manage to use leverage to their potential are often those with years of experience in trading, and an excellent knowledge of the system. Always start out small if you're a beginner, as you will win some and lose some. Don't gnaw on more than you are ready for.

Silly as it may sound; overconfident traders believe that they can make it happen in the market, instead of waiting to see what the market can offer. Thinking that they are bigger than the market (and sometimes, even the universe), they often fight the market trend in trying to catch the tops and bottoms.

While humble traders acknowledge that sometimes, the trade just isn't there, traders who are overconfident display impatience. Afraid that they will miss out on opportunities, they grab any that come along, even if they may miss out on what is most important - the money.

Optimism is the enemy of the rationale trader. Not every tree is worth biting off. Rather than following imaginary predictions based on 'gut feel', focus on trading rules - this is why I advocate all traders to keep a comprehensive checklist, and monitor them to ensure that they keep to it. I would also encourage starting with a smaller percentage of capital in live trading, so as to get acquainted with adhering to trading rules.

Practise, practise and practise more. Train yourself to view trading as a regimental process. With continuous practice, the process will become ingrained in you, and overconfidence can then be easily kept in check.

> *Losses follow those who do not respect the market and try to bite off more than they can chew. Follow your trading plan and rules faithfully until you learn to respect it.*

Cardinal Sin 2: Egoism

The worst trader you'll ever meet is your ego. According to Tom Baldwin, the bond trader investor and founder of the Baldwin Group, *'the best traders have no ego. Swallow your pride, and get out of the losses'*, he advises.

"I need to win!"

Everyone likes to win. It naturally feels good when we are rewarded with profits after a good trade that is backed by sufficient research and hard work. You want to show to the whole world that you've conquered the biggest trees.

However, there is a difference between ego trading and successful trading. *Successful traders* <u>*want*</u> *their trades to do well. Egoistic lemming traders* <u>*need*</u> *their trades to do well, be it to boost their self-esteem, or to prove a point.*

How many of the following describes how you feel towards your trading position?

- I need to win back what I've lost.
- I need to prove to myself and others that the previous failed trade will be my last
- I need this trade to start off a winning streak

Any one of the above feelings is very dangerous indeed. When you equate your trading position to your self-esteem, you are susceptible to depression and euphoria along with the rise and fall of the market.

If you start to feel really down because of a dissatisfactory trade, you've traded more than just your money, but also your self-esteem. When we trade with our ego, it's akin to having a psychological time bomb in our heads, ready to trigger any time.

We tend to be more affected by ego in trading when our personal lives are not going as well. To avoid this pitfall, invest your self-esteem not in the market, but in places that deserve it - your family and friends, career, religion and even the things you enjoy doing in your leisure time.

You'll find that not only will your chosen trades start taking a turn for the better, so does the quality of your life.

"How will others view me?"

Another problem that arises out of egoistic trading comes when you're afraid of appearing 'stupid'. You let your market decisions be restricted or affected by worry of how others will see you.

Warren Buffett has this to say about independent thinking: You're neither right nor wrong because others agree with you. You're right because your facts and reasoning are right.

Indeed, during the boom of high-tech stocks, Buffett refused to get involved, even though millions of investors were getting rich. His shareholders criticised him, and publication headlines bombarded Buffett for his inactivity. "Is Buffett Washed Up?" "What's Wrong, Warren?" and "A Three Decade Legend Loses Some Luster."

Later, the dot com bubble burst, and the same millions of investors went bankrupt.

He who laughs last, laughs best. Never let what others say or do get to you. Be assured in the facts and your reasoning to come to a firm stand, then hold to your position.

After all, it is not whether you're right or wrong that ultimately matters, but how much money you make or lose.

Never trade with your self-esteem, and always hold firm to a position that is backed by your research and good sense.

Cardinal Sin 3: Perfectionism

All our lives, we have been taught to strive for perfection, be it in academics by our well-meaning parents or in other aspects. While perfectionism is crucial for some industries and jobs (think architecture and brain surgeons), it is fatal for traders.

The Perfectionist Trader

It's easy to spot the perfectionist; he or she sets unrealistically high and sometimes, absurd standards for one or more aspects of his or her life, believing that everything would fall into place if they just achieved that. These people are often driven and strive hard at what they believe in.

Of course, all is good when they get what they want. Problem is, their impossible goals are rarely met. They then go into self-doubt, and believe themselves to be not good enough.

Perfectionists believe that they have to be the best in order to gain approval from others. These people often do not feel loved and worthy as they are, and hence rationalise and disguise perfectionism as a drive for improvement.

Such a mindset is not only harmful to our psychological well-being, but just as detrimental to a trader's wallet. Often, when the pain of a losing trade far exceeds the joy of a winning one, it's because the perfectionist in us is at work.

Perfectionists are unable to handle even small losses due to their need for perfection, and end up winding up with larger losses. Instead of cutting losses early and letting profits run, perfectionists do the opposite thing. They enter trades at the wrong times, stay for too long, then exit at the wrong times.

Perfectionist traders are likely to overtrade, as they feel internal pressure to make profits to recoup previous losses. Driven by the desire to succeed, they also tend to turn a blind eye to market events.

They are achievement-oriented, often setting performance goals for themselves that revolve around profits. This can result in performance anxiety that affects rational thinking.

To avoid unnecessary performance anxiety, replace all your performance goals with process goals. Instead of aiming to make say, $100,000 annually, set goals to follow your trading plan based on position sizes, entries and exits.

Striking a Balance

Unfortunately for perfectionists (and for the rest of us), there can be no perfection in the trading world. If you flit from systems to systems, hoping to find The Strategy that will guarantee 100% winnings, then you are doomed to fail, for it is a given that you must experience losses along the way.

Trading is not about perfection, but probability and progress. Even technical analysis is built on probability. Instead of demanding 100% winnings, put probability in your favour, and success will follow.

See the mini checklist below. How many are you guilty of?

- "I should've known better." When the trade didn't go as you planned or imagined, you reproach yourself for not having made a wise move.

- "I wasn't meticulous enough." When the trade has made some profit, you start scouring other portions of the move you did not make but should have.

- "It was so obvious it was going to be a bull run." When the trade has profited tremendously, you blame yourself for not having put in more capital.

This is perfectionism in action. Note that there is a fine line between motivation to improve and deflating your own confidence. If you find yourself guilty of one or more of the above, you might just be overindulging the perfectionist in you. It's as though you're subconsciously finding a way to "bash" yourself up, isn't it? And while you're busy bashing yourself for your 'stupidity', other better trades have slipped past you.

Not only does negative self-reproach make you unhappy, it deeply undermines your confidence, which in turn harms your trading DNA. When you focus on the portion of the move that you should or should not have done, relative to your expectations of yourself, financial losses become failures, and the most admirable successes transform into defeats.

Trying to achieve perfectionism is demoralising to any trader, takes away the joy of trading, and can even lead to depression. Rather than thinking of gaining acceptance through performance, realise that your performance is in no way related to your self-worth and is but a temporary state.

It is more important that you focus on identifying what caused this temporary failure. A journal is a great start to helping you recognise what you did wrong in the trade, so you don't repeat it.

The next time you feel miserable after a trade which you felt could've been better, turn to the last page of your journal, and write down exactly how you feel, leaving an empty row of space between each line of words.

******

It was utterly stupid of me… how could I have not guessed that the trade would continue to rise? It was so obvious… Now I have just caused myself to 'lose' so much money for nothing! You fool!

******

Then go to sleep, and read it the next day. Underline all the phrases and sentences that you wouldn't ever think of saying to your closest friend when he or she is feeling down, and rewrite them.

******

Hmmm… if I had waited a couple more days, it might have been even better, but hey… I was just being over-cautious. Now, there'll definitely be better trades coming up, and this time, I'll access my options even more carefully!

******

The trick is to address what went wrong, and how you can do better in future. Realise that to err is human (and also admittedly costly at times), but hey, a bruised ego may cost you more in the near future. Treat yourself with respect, and your stock performance will follow suit!

Life can be lived forward, but can only be understood backwards. Here are some steps that will help anyone become a happier trader:

- Set realistic and achievable trading goals based on process, not just results.
- Enjoy the entire process of trading
- Free yourself from self-blame and learn from your mistakes
- Lastly, remember that your self-worth is not measured by your wins and losses, and that losses are but a temporary state that can be overcome

---

To err is costly now, but a bruised ego may cost you more in future. Rather than demand perfection on each trade, strive for long-term and sustainable performance.

Remember, trading is a marathon, not a sprint.

Together, they're deadlier!

Note that the above-mentioned 3 vices are not independent of each other. A lemming trader can display all 3 traits - taking a trading position out of overconfidence, then refusing to let go because of his stubborn ego. He then falls into misery and depression when he does not meet their perfectionist (and unrealistic) goals.

Sounds like a vicious cycle, doesn't it? The good news is that you can turn these deadly vices around with your discipline. When you make conscious effort to develop yourself emotionally, socially and professionally, you'll find that not only will you start earning more money in the market; you'll earn many more brownie points with people around you as well.

The Vicious Cycle of Deadly Vices

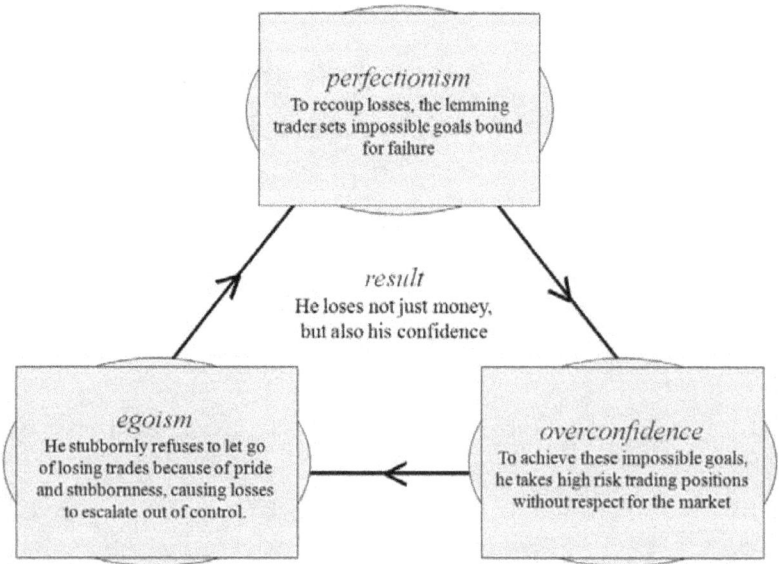

perfectionism
To recoup losses, the lemming trader sets impossible goals bound for failure

result
He loses not just money, but also his confidence

egoism
He stubbornly refuses to let go of losing trades because of pride and stubbornness, causing losses to escalate out of control.

overconfidence
To achieve these impossible goals, he takes high risk trading positions without respect for the market

go on, we're all DOING it

PHASE II

Herd Mentality

Lemmings are known to follow the herd. Like lemmings, we humans live in a community. This means we inevitably get affected by what other lemming traders talk about or how other lemming traders are behaving.

At such a stage, the lemming traders are in a very bullish emotional mode. They run in a herd towards the cliffs, confident that they are safe in numbers. The traders grow more confident and buy and buy. Unfortunately, majority is not always right in trading (in fact the opposite is often quite true).

More often than not, it becomes a bull market in no time.

What I'm trying to say is, there's no way you can avoid market chatter. It certainly doesn't make any sense to uproot and trade at a deserted mountain where you'd be unaffected by others (not to mention the lack of internet connection and inconvenience).

Instead, I'm going to show you how to avoid getting influenced by the lemming traders around *The Right Frame of Mind*. You'll be surprised how far having the right frame of mind will take you.

The Right Frame of Mind

When trying to improve as a trader, most people look outward; but the only way to succeed is to look inward.

Dr. Charles B. Schaap, Author of *Invest with Success*

Having the right frame of mind is crucial if you want to move away from the lemming herd, improve and make consistent profits from the market. Here, we'll explore the 4 correct mindsets to adopt as an individual towards **1)** trading on the whole, **2)** before a trade, **3)** during the trade and **4)** after the trade.

1. Trading on the Whole

I am going to briefly introduce you to the powerful idea of *Attributional Bias*, a popular social psychology theory that has been applied to trading by Brett N. Steenbarger, author of *The Psychology of Trading*. It will greatly help you understand how and why we tend to gravitate towards emotional over rational trading.

Attributions refer to the qualities that we place on ourselves and the explanations we give for events, in order to make sense of the world. For instance, we tend to attribute our winning trades to our skills, and our losing trades to ill luck.

This self-serving attributional bias is what puts most traders at risk of irrational trading. Rather than looking inward for the fundamental personality traits and mindset (like impulsiveness and market revenge) that caused the losing outcome, they tend to look to situational forces (like blaming it on unexpected market turns).

As the saying goes, even a clock that does not work is right twice a day. Most traders will always attribute wins to their own credit, and losses to bad luck.

Lemming traders never look inward; they always blame the ambiguous "others" for their losses - the big players and other institutions that 'must be manipulating the market'. These people never learn from their mistakes, and never become successful either. They mostly end up as angry, frustrated lemmings who plunge to their sorry ends when they try and take revenge on the market, and harming their own portfolio (and mental) health as a result.

These lemming traders also tend to give themselves too much credit when trades go their way, believing that they 'made it happen' with their skills and ability. Overconfident, they then go for increased capital and trading frequency, which inevitably results in more losses than wins over time. They then conveniently blame others for their losses, and the vicious cycle repeats itself.

To avoid falling into such a self-serving mindset, we must first recognise the difference between a bad and losing trade, and a good and winning trade.

A bad trade is one that lacks in objective and research, while a losing trade simply means one that lost money. A good trade is one that is placed upon research and insight, while a winning trade is one that makes money. Chance alone can result in bad trades becoming winning trades, and good trades becoming losing ones.

Lemming traders who conveniently blame their losses on chance can never learn, even after a decade of trading. On the other hand, traders who choose to ignore this element of chance might end up over-attributing losses and wins to themselves. This illusion of control is what causes depression and euphoria in the market, and distracts most traders from consistent profits.

Many traders spend a lifetime trying to figure out market movements and technical charts, but never once try to understand how they think towards the financial markets in the first place. Learn to become more aware of your own self-serving attributional bias. This will free up your psychological mindset, allowing you to focus all your energies on trading rationally and profitably.

You can attain peak trader performance by meeting the following 5Cs via the tips given below:
- Composure
- Concentration
- Confidence
- Coping with Challenges
- Cohesion

Composure

Staying calm in stressful situations is of utmost importance. Some tips to help you stay calm include:
- Not counting your profits and losses whilst still in the trade
- Take a breather when you feel your breathing becoming faster
- Learn to relax by taking deep breaths
- Verbally tell yourself to "stay calm" and "remain steady"

Concentration

Staying focused during trading will get you far. To improve your concentration:
- Trade only when you have rested well
- Never multi-task when you are trading; msn messenger is a no-no
- Take a short break every now and then; the average human attention span is only 20 minutes
- Keep your trading strategy as simple as it takes to be effective

Confidence

Self-doubt can hinder you from attaining trading success. Pay attention to the following:

- Understand that losses are part and parcel of trading
- Do not flit from strategy to strategy; keep to one sensible plan
- Practise risk management and keep each trade small
- Stay positive and tell yourself that you are capable of success
- Identify your strengths and motivations for trading

Coping with Challenges

How prone are you to revenge trading? Here are pointers to guard yourself against this fatal mistake:

- Remind yourself that the market is bigger than you
- Recognise that even good trades can turn out to be losing trades
- Be patient
- Ego has no part to play in trading.
- Learn from your mistakes by jotting them down in a journal

Cohesion

Negative thoughts will only work against you. Develop a winning mindset:

- Keep the thoughts positive
- Focus on what you want, not the reverse
- Know your own weaknesses
- Avoid being greedy; this may turn wins into losses

Understand that chance alone can result in bad trades becoming winning trades, and good trades becoming losing ones.

Avoid under or over-attributing wins or losses to external events, and look inwards to improve as a trader.

---

2. Before a Trade

If you want to be a successful trader, you must make sure you are not denying reality before starting out on any trade.

The denial here refers to trying to shut out any unpleasant related events or personal traits we have that are less-than-ideal, such as our losses, mistakes, stubbornness or impulsiveness.

We all have strengths and weaknesses, and being truthful about ourselves is the key to becoming a great trader. Much as denial is part of human nature, ignoring and running away from reality will not get you anywhere (or rich). This refusal to accept and address our problems distracts our focus from the action of price movements during the actual trading process. Denial is lethal and costly, for a clouded mind is unable to read the market as accurately as a mind who 'knows thyself'.

Learn to acknowledge what you have been trying to avoid confronting all this while. Open your trading journal, and start writing down all the issues and ideas that you are unable to accept or handle, such as sheer chance causing a badly placed trade to be profitable, indicators that can never be 100% accurate, and so forth.

Then access which points are inevitable due to the unpredictable nature of the market, and just recognise that you have to accept them someday - so why not now. Then tick those points that are caused by your own psychological barriers. These are the thoughts you can control and change.

Instead of focusing your energy in denial, shift these energies to acknowledging that your doubts and flaws exist, and then improving on them by getting to the core of the issues.

For instance, common flaws among lemming traders include charging mindlessly in one direction and not changing with the fast-moving market. They are also not able to maintain consistent profits. The first problem often stems from character traits like stubbornness and ego, not being observant enough of market trends, but only follows the herd blindly. The latter is often a result of overconfidence and emotional trading.

Another example is not being able to accept that the market is always right, and that anything can happen. Accept this fact and set stop losses.

Think about the other aspects that can distract you from seeing the market with a clear mind, and confront them with the knowledge that you will improve upon what you have picked out. You'll become a better trader in the process. Only after performing these self-checks can we begin trading proper, with greater success.

TIP: Much as psychology is important, do not neglect your physiological aspect. If you are hungry, sleep-deprived, feeling unwell or having a hangover, it only makes sense that you halt all trading activities and resume after you have fully recovered.

Accept that every trader has his own unique flaws and unpleasant trading experiences, and work on improving them instead of evading these issues. Ignoring them will not make the recurrent problems go away.

3. During the Trade

A trader can plan and research for days before a trade, but if he doesn't carry out his plan during the course of the trading but instead make a mad plunge, it is as good as burning up the time and effort spent beforehand.

Often, when we plan the trade but don't trade the plan, it is because we made the trade about ourselves, instead of about the market. Imagine fantasising about how much you will be making even before entering a trade. Or how you lost the last time, and how much more you could have done.

With so much psychological energies focused on yourself, how much rationality can you devote to your trading decision? Remember, it is not so much of how much of a winner or loser you are, but rather, how you interpret the market and how well you control your own emotions and self-talk during the trade itself. It's never about yourself or your self-esteem, but the market and its fluctuations.

If you immerse in your own feelings of frustration, anger, euphoria, guilt or hope, you become enveloped and shrouded by a veil that prevents you from seeing the sea of markets what they are.

Never focus on the outcome of the trading, but always the process. If you pay too much attention to winning, you'll get distracted by the prospects and lose sight of the actual process needed to get you there.

When you focus solely on winning, you are feeding your fear, greed, overconfidence, self-blame, self-esteem and fantasies. This is when you might end up hating the market, and perform revenge trading. Or, you might feel overly self-conscious, and decrease your ability to be rational about the trades you make.

In turn, you end up blaming yourself for the losing trades, and the cycle repeats.

Do not blame the cold harsh market or yourself. Be cool and collected, by focusing on the plan you have agreed on beforehand, and stick with it.

Never act out your internal conflicts and emotions in the market. Instead, choose to indulge in fulfilling activities that enhance yourself physically, socially, and mentally.

When you feel fulfilled outside of trading, you are much less likely to build your identity and expectations of yourself around the market, hence freeing your burdened mind to stay with your initial plan.

As Alexander Elder, a professional stock trader would say, a good trader watches his or her capital as successfully as a professional scuba-diver watches his or her air supply. Never succumb to your own emotions and end up gambling with your capital during the trade.

A financial market is the combined result of millions of lemming traders responding to information, misinformation, whim and fancy. This is why there are unlimited opportunities for you to both abuse and benefit from it.

Always trade with a proper plan to avoid emotions getting in the way, and never focus on winning, but focus instead on the process.

4. After the Trade

It is all too tempting to access your trading performance based on the results. When you lose a trade, the first thought that appears in your mind is likely to be, "my system must not be effective enough", or "I just knew it was going to be a mistake!"

Instead of shifting the blame outwards or crying over spilt milk like lemming traders do, the most successful traders look inwards to dig for the nature of their errors, then improve on them the next time round.

This is that little difference that separates the 5% of traders who manage to make consistent profits from the market from the lemmings. Instead of dwelling on mistakes, this 5% treat errors as a learning opportunity.

Winning traders never forget the mistakes they committed; to them, a mistake is a blessing in disguise that allows them to do it even better the next time. Believe it or not, this tiny difference is what separates this 5% of successful traders from the mediocre.

This means, fortunately, that we do not have to be the brightest man in our neighbourhood to be a good trader. We simply need the humility to admit our mistakes, then learn from them. It's just as well, since you can't hide your failures in trading when your portfolio clearly reflects your performance.

However, take note of the approach with which you 'learn'. Traders who continue learning to improve and progress in technique becomes eventually better and better, but lemming traders who focus solely on learning to win often end up at a stagnant level where they stop improving for fear of losing.

Traders who choose to blame his losses on external events will never learn from mistakes. As Victor Sperandeo, well-known Wall Street stock trader and speculator puts it, rationalisation is a guaranteed road to ultimate failure.

TIP: Never boast about your wins, tempting as it may be. This is because it is never easy to keep up one's reputation in the turbulent financial markets. When you boast about your huge profits, you often end up having to keep up with your appearances to fellow lemmings, and the stress on our ego often causes the sharpest trader to make irrational decisions.

Remember that huge profits go to the humble, and give up building a reputation. Simply admit that you are having some difficulty achieving the same results as before, and refocus your energies in the right places.

Never blame your losses on external events; choose instead to look inwards and improve on yourself as a trader. Learn with the aim not solely on winning, but on trading better the next time round.

unseen forces make gob
do the unthinkable

PHASE III

The Plunge

As the stampede nears the cliff, it becomes even more chaotic when the lemmings sense danger near. The lemmings behave like they are out of control and possessed. They become irrational; you could sniff the fear.

In the same fashion, lemming traders start to realise from the mounting losses that something is not quite right. What happens next is that they unload all their huge losing positions at the same time. Armed with no lifevests or buoys, the lemming traders make a blind leap of fatal faith and take the plunge into icy cold waters.

It was what happened in the Asian Economic Crisis in 1997. Now we know the lemming traders were behind it.

Don't fall into the emotional trap of lemming traders. Enhance your trading discipline when you read the following chapter: *Emotions - your worst enemies.*

Emotions: Your Worst Enemies

Trading Stocks is simple mathematics. 2 + 2 = 4,
but our greed makes it 5 and our panic makes it 3.

Anonymous

Issac Newton once said, *"I can calculate the motions of the heavenly bodies but not the madness of people."*

Note the gravity (pun unintended) of what Newton said. This madness he speaks of is caused none other than by human emotions. In fact, market movements to under and over-valued extremes are a result of human emotions. It is all too easy to fall prey to our own emotional whims.

While there are many traits that are required for a trader to become successful, the ability to control one's own emotions has to be one of the most crucial. After all, a trader is often forced to make fast decisions when he enters and exits the market in real time. There is no place for emotions to affect one's frame of mind.

Emotional trading is lethal. Never participate in this folly; only profit from it. Here's how:

1. Fear and Greed

The two key emotions that a trader needs to master in the right combination to succeed are fear and greed.

Fear is an unpleasant feeling of excessive anticipation and awareness of danger. Greed manifests as excessive desire, and is what former Federal Reserve chairman Alan Greenspan puts it, an "irrational exuberance". (Excesses are never good!)

The results of fear and greed are especially potent in modern day, where high-speed information processing and cheap personalised trading capabilities allow us to trade at the click of a mouse.

With virtual demo trading accounts, it is all too easy to stay with our intended plan, as the risk of real loss is non-existent. Once beginners move into real-life trading, however, personal emotion starts to interfere, and rationality goes out the window.

While fear and greed are the two most common emotions that can wreak havoc on an otherwise profitable trading career, the greatest problem here is not the emotions; in fact many successful traders are very emotional people.

The problem does not come from experiencing these emotions, but the way one chooses to react to them. Good traders feel the same emotions, but choose not to dwell upon them. Lemming traders let the negative emotions get to them and start dashing even faster in panic.

Good traders recognise these emotions and master them to prevent their emotions from affecting their presence of mind. The even better ones put these emotions to good use; they have enough fear of the market to respect it, without thinking they are always right. They also possess a healthy level of greed to allow winning trades to run during the rare occasions.

If you are unable to let go of fear and greed after recognising them, you will get caught up in a vicious cycle of self-doubt, causing your logical mind and cognitive ability to be affected. Before long, you find yourself in deep waters. Without even realising it, you would have taken a blind plunge together with the other lemming traders. But if you are able to remove the emotional element before you put on a trading position, you're on your way to a good start.

Emotions compete with your
cognitive, rational ability to access the market.

1a.   Fear and Greed in a Losing Trade

Recall your last losing trade. What did you do? Did you hold on to your trades for fear that they will bounce back? Or did you greedily hold on because you wished to recoup the losses with this losing trade, although prices are fast falling? Not very sound logic at play here, as you can see.

Ironically, the more serious you are about trading, the more susceptible you are to emotions that drive you to making poor decisions. This is because you see your trading decisions as an extension of yourself, and hence get more upset when things do not go your expected way.

Learn to cut losses fast. One way to get around our fear and greed is to make sure that our trading goals are set not on money, but on the process of trading. Use tools like Stop Losses and Conditional Orders. Continually access if the reasoning behind your initial position still stands - if for some reason it doesn't, exit or at least reduce your position.

Remember that one bad trading decision does not make you a bad person, nor a bad trader. Every successful trader has had his or her fair share of losses, taken in stride.

On the other hand, bad news about a trade may not necessary be that negative, though it probably sends many a scared lemming trader to liquidate their positions. While he may avoid losses this way, he may also miss out on gains. In such cases, it might be helpful to understand what fear is.

Fear is a human reaction to what we perceive as a threat to what we care about (in this case our money). Thus, it is a good idea to note down specifically what is it that scares you, why it does, and what you do as a result. Understand how fear affects you and take measures to avoid these natural responses.

By quantifying your fear into facts and making it less of an unknown, you will be better able to handle fear when you feel it the next time round. You can isolate and pinpoint what it is that makes your heart beat faster, and access if it is a justified fear or an overrated panic attack.

The next time before you start a trade, check yourself to reduce any pressure that can escalate your emotions. Do you have any unrealistic expectations towards your trading performance?

Perform the 'Must Test'. If there are any 'must' expectations of yourself - "I must recoup all my losses in this round" or "I must make X amount of money", then don't trade that day. Sometimes, your best trades and investments are the ones you don't make.

Millions saw the apple fall, but Newton asked why. Instead of focusing on your losses, understand the root cause of the loss.

1b. Fear and Greed in a Winning trade

Now, what about when your trade is in a wining position? There are many who would greedily refuse to exit even when the profit position is reached.

Greed is never easy to overcome. After all, the two birds in the tree always look better than the one already in your hand. The next they know, all their winnings have been wiped out by a sudden market change. Recognise that greed is an instinctive emotion in humans to push us to do even better, and overcome it by basing your trading moves on a sensible trading plan.

It is also most tempting to grab the profits before it has reached your profit position. Fear is at work here. You are afraid that there will be a market change and your trade will turn into a losing one.

In fact, your fear manifests itself physiologically. Your heart beats faster, and you find your breathing shallower. Before you know it, you have exited your trade. You then heave a sigh of momentary relief.

Do you realise something? You have made your decision not with money management in mind, but rather to relieve your emotional stress. This self-defeating mentality can prevent you from cashing out a much bigger gain.

Before a trade, you are relaxed and calm. However, once you enter a trade, the prospect of winning or losing money gets to you, and clouds your better judgment. This is why it is important that you have a sound trading plan that you can stick to, throughout the course of your trade, and follow closely to.

You may have been subconsciously influenced by countless stories of gamblers, who, upon winning some money, lost it all after refusing to leave the table. However, realise that your profit position is set based on much research (it should have!), and is not comparable to gambling.

Have faith, and start developing the discipline to cut losses early, and let profiting trades run. Otherwise, your carefully calculated reward-risk ratio will be ruined, and you'll be losing money in the long run.

In a winning trade, stick with your initial trading plan!
Don't fall prey to greed or emotional stress.

1c. Fear and Greed in an Elevated Position

Another interesting thing to note is that while some traders may have conquered their emotions and performance anxiety at a certain level of capital, these same people panic when the capital size is increased.

It takes two minutes to cook an egg in a boiling pan of water. When you increase the number of eggs to ten, it takes two minutes, still, and the procedure remains the same. It is hence illogical for us to suffer more performance anxiety when more money is at stake, be it due to leverages or increase in capital.

If you are unable to handle a significant increase in capital, don't. Most of us are aware of this and do not attempt to do so, which is actually a good thing. After all, it is much, much wiser to go for gradual increments, rather than a sudden jump in capital.

> *One egg or ten, it takes the same two minutes and procedure to cook. Stay calm in the face of increased capital, or don't increase it at all, until you are ready.*

1d. Fear of Regret

By regret, we're referring to the emotions that lemming traders feel upon realising that a bad trading decision was made. Because they do not want to make the loss official or admit that the decision was faulty, their judgment becomes impaired and they refuse to sell. They charge on despite knowing that what awaits is a high cliff.

Fear of regret usually operates in a vicious cycle, as attempts to avoid feeling this regret can lead on to even more regret later on.

To avoid falling into this trap, use this little trick: Ask yourself if you would consider trading this position again after selling it. If the answer is no, sell it immediately.

A strange phenomenon is how lemming traders with herd mentality tend to feel less bad and embarrassed when they lose in popular stocks that 'everyone's buying', as opposed to less popular or known stocks. Fear of regret could be the explanation - some traders feel that by trading in popular stocks, they reduce the possibility that they would invest in a stock they might regret later by rationalising the false logic that if everyone's doing it, it must be right.

Obviously, it is not so in the world of trading. Following the majority may pay off in some cases, but never in trading and investing.

Fear of regret operates in a vicious cycle. If you are holding a position that you will not want to buy again after selling, close it immediately.

2. Self talk during the Trade

Ever heard of the saying "you are your worst enemy?" That is most true in terms of trading, more so during the trading process itself.

Whether you are aware of it, we talk to ourselves all the time - be it to rationalise, sort out some ideas, self-blame, or reaffirm our beliefs. Most of us do it silently; some choose to do it aloud, much to the amusement of others.

Self-talk is actually the manifestation of our subconscious mind at work. The subconscious is a very powerful thing. Whenever our subconscious mind has to decide between logic and our deep-rooted emotions, the latter always wins.

This is what we refer to as bringing past bad experiences with is when we trade. If your self-talk is negative and defeated, it could be because you have been deeply affected by a bad decision you once made. Learn from successful traders. They've all had their fair share of losses, but they take it in stride, aware that losses are part and parcel of trading.

More often than not, self-talk is the main culprit behind why we fail to adhere to our initial trading plan. It is as though our self-talk has taken a life of its own, and we are completely hijacked and driven away from our original route of intended course.

How we talk to ourselves during the trading process and after-monitoring will greatly influence how we manage that trade. Take note of your self-talk the next time you place a trade. How much of it is market-focused, and how much of it is driven by illogical fear and greed?

Do you cut winning trades short because you subconsciously believe you are not capable of larger profits? Or worse, become stubborn in position, causing little losses to escalate into big ones?

That is why it is so crucial to recognise and separate negative self-talk from constructive ones and control it, or better still, abolish this negativity all together.

Negative self-talk interferes with our right brain that is responsible for rational thinking, causing our analytical processing to be less accurate than it should be. This is when you are most likely to make unwise decisions that may jeopardise that trade.

To ease any unnecessary pressure from your trading performance that can trigger negative self-talk, always focus on process goals, not monetary end goals. Instead of aiming to earn say, $3000, aim to limit your losses to two ticks if you're a scalper, or release trades only when the trailing stop is hit.

Whenever you feel affected by the price movements and realise that your thoughts are turning negative, step away from your screen. Go to another room, take a few deep breaths and perform some stretches. Then slowly access your options. Only return to the screen when you've firmly decided on your course of action.

Another way of handling self-talk is to steer it towards positive, constructive thoughts. Know that so long as you trade the right way, profits will come naturally.

After a losing trade, remind yourself that this is just a trade out of many others. As long as you have made sufficient preparation, you'll be rewarded with a good reward-risk ratio from the all the trades you undertook.

Even for a successful trader, not all trades are winning trades. It's normal to suffer bleeding and feel out of tune with the market at times. When this happens to you, simply scale down the capital exposure to reduce the chances of negativity creeping in.

Moreover, negative self-talk tends to go into overdrive when you have much to lose. With leverages and hedging available freely to us, it's easy to trade beyond what we're capable of handling. Never spend more than we have. Spending more than what you're earning will burden any trader's mind.

If you're a beginner, trade with an amount of money that you can afford to lose, but large enough for you to feel the pain if you do.

Never trade more than what you're comfortable with. A good gauge is to assume the worst-case scenario. If you're unable to handle that, then don't go through with the trade. In short, avoid playing with 'scared money'.

Lastly, to be a successful trader, you must believe that consistent earnings are possible. You can never achieve something that you already believe to be impossible.

Despite many winning traders being very successful, they do not live an extravagant life. They know that they can earn money in trading because they do not have the pressure of needing that sum of money. Lemming traders who are desperate in making money from trading can never be successful long term.

Avoid negative self-talk. Remember that profits will come naturally so do not fall into the vicious trap of self-blame.

By the time gob
realises, it's too late

PHASE IV

The Regretful Realisation

There comes a point in time where the lemming (who has taken the plunge) realises he is going to drown. He tries to clamour back on dry land but considering that cliffs can range countless metres in height, it is an impossible task. It is oh-so-easy to jump from the cliff down, but almost impossible to get back up. Think about it. It takes no effort to reduce a portfolio of say, USD5,000 to USD100, but it would take much to raise a portfolio of USD100 to USD5,000.

After the lemming trader realises his mistake (often too late), there is simply no capital to make a return. The lemming trader, left with very little capital, makes the last feeble attempts to waddle in the financial markets. As he struggles to his death, he is unnoticed in the huge herd of the other lemming traders.

We must not forget that all lemmings are actually strong swimmers. They drown because they are overcome by the incessant waves of vast market forces in the sea.

Now, the sea of financial markets can be a scary place if you're not prepared. Even the strongest of swimmers need buoys they can rely on, because their swimming skills can be no match for the power of nature (or the markets).

Prevention is better than cure. That's why we all need strong trading systems that we can fall back on, so we never need to find ourselves in a state of regretful realisation later. Here, I'll guide you on selecting the best trading system for yourself in *The Trading System*, because one size of life vests never fits all. Remember to stay armed.

The Trading System

"The market may be bad, but I slept like a baby last night. I woke up every hour and cried."

Anonymous

If you trade and have difficulty sleeping at night (despite having tried everything from sleeping pills to hypnosis), you may have chosen the wrong trading instrument or system.

How do you then decide which trading instrument or system is best for you? Most traders choose trading instruments and systems based on which they feel are more profitable, reputable etc. While there's nothing wrong with that, it would be good to take into consideration a couple of other things.

Think about your personality, beliefs and behaviours. Are you a patient or impatient person? Indecisive or firm? Shark diving or book reading for you? Did you read this book in chorological order or skipped some chapters?

Each individual is vastly different, and the chosen system should be one that suits the trader, and not the other way round. Besides your character traits, you should also consider other factors such as the amount of time you are willing and able to devote, and the level of risk you are comfortable with.

These major considerations in choosing a suitable system will go a long way to increase your profits later on.

Basically, traders become millionaires when they have confidence in themselves and their system. They stick with the plan and believe what they are doing is true. They trust their edge. They do not follow what others are doing blindly, but choose to understand their personality in order to develop their own style of trading. Some like fading while others like to follow trends, but no matter the preference, these traders have developed the right mindset to help them stay cool in the game.

Open your mind to different trading instruments and systems. They all have their pros and cons that will suit differing personalities. Keeping in mind what type of trader you are, choose one, and stay strictly to the rules of the game you have chosen to play.

While studying the market helps you become a better trader, studying yourself enables you to play up your strengths and maximise them, and become aware of your weaknesses to minimise them. This will bring your trading portfolio to heights not achievable by a mere focus on the market alone.

> *Always choose a trading instrument and system that*
> *suit your personality, risk appetite and time horizon for best results.*

The Importance of a Suitable Trading System

Even if you are not considering trading full-time, part-time trading can easily supplement your income by up to thousands or more, if you follow the right methods with discipline.

The point is this: no matter what trading instrument you eventually settle on, be sure to find out all you can beforehand about the benefits and disadvantages of each to ensure that it's a good fit with your personality.

For instance, even currency pairs in forex have their own unique characteristics. Volatility, average daily range, liquidity and specific patterns are just some of the factors that differentiate one currency pair from another.

If you prefer short-term investments, more volatile pairs are more suitable. If you are one who is uncomfortable with rapid changes in prices, a more stable currency pair would work better for you. Choose strategies that go hand in hand with the characteristics of that particular trading pair for best results.

Remember, one size never fits all in the world of trading. Choose a trading instrument and system much more carefully than you would consider which car model or frilly dress to purchase! Many have come to me for help on selecting trading styles that is most appropriate for their personality and constraints.

There is no perfect system that will guarantee only winning trades, but a good system tells you when it's time to cut your losses.

Over the years, I have developed a proprietary system known as the *Strategy Creation Process*™ to help myself analyse the forex charts, maximise my wins and improve the way I trade by constantly adapting to the ever-changing forex market. Because of its effectiveness and the fact that it is catered to Asian hours and suitable for busy executives, the method later gained popularity.

Renowned in the Forex Trading industry and featured in various press media, *Strategy Creation Process*™ is the proprietary system of formulating new and existing strategies through the comprehensive dissection of the currency market price movements through live market analysis.

Note about Risk

You may have heard of the saying 'low risk low returns, high risk high returns'. The truth is, risk need not and should not be high, for it can be easily regulated with a sensible adherence to a reliable trading system.

A licensed pilot flying a plane is likely to be at lower risk of danger than an amateur on a bicycle. Likewise, even seemingly 'safe' trades widely acclaimed by public can be risky if you are not educated and well-versed in trading. The same goes for seemingly high risk trading instruments like trading currencies; while forex has a reputation for being high risk, it is no more riskier than one entering a 'safe' trade blindfolded.

Be educated, train yourself, and your risks in whichever instrument you choose will be greatly controlled and minimised. There is no shortcut to becoming a successful trader!

Succeeding with the Right Plan

Never be like an unprepared lemming trader. As the Chinese saying goes, if you must play, decide on three things at the start: the rules of the game, the stakes, and the quitting time. Here I have stated and explained what you should be considering before plunging into a trade.

1. Having a Plan

Whichever trading instrument and strategy you choose, remember this: Fail to plan and you are planning to fail. The major reason why many traders fail to become successful is the lack of a written trading plan.

While having a plan does not guarantee immediate returns on profit (especially if you chose the wrong strategy), it ensures that you can record and rectify any issues quickly. Documenting your trading allows you to avoid making costly mistakes repeatedly.

In fact, the best trading plan is one that is not only proven effective, but also evolves and changes over time with the market. Continually evaluate your plan to keep it consistent with the dynamic market.

A good plan should also be a reflection of yourself - your sleeping habits, risk appetite, and financial goals. Never copy the trading plans of others lock, stock and barrel, successful as they may seem. What works for one may be another's poison.

2. Timing

One of the mistakes that beginner and lemming traders make is trying to ride on absolute tops and bottoms. While they may succeed a couple of times, trying to be too precise about a prediction may cause them major losses in the end. Leave "absolute" to the vodka makers. Kick this habit fast.

To buy near the bottoms and sell near the tops, you need utter discipline and emotional control. You are your worst enemy; after all no one pointed a gun at the lemming to force him to jump.

Another timing problem with lemming traders is being too premature on taking the plunge and entering positions. Learn to be patient, both in terms of profit target reached and also entering trades. Sometimes weeks can go by without any positive trade signals. Always ensure that everything is in place before entering a trade.

As Linda Bradford Raschke, President of LBR Group, suggested, it's better to have the wrong idea and good timing than the right idea and bad timing.

Always follow a strict checklist to determine if a trade is worth entering. If you are uncertain when is a good time, get your hands on a reliable checklist. If in doubt, do not trade.

3. Entry and Exit Strategies

Many a trader know what to buy, but are unsure of when and where to exit.

Before entering a trade, always set realistic risk-reward ratios and targets. Think about your minimum risk-reward ratio. If you desire a potential profit twice the risk, then your goal should be a $2 profit for the one dollar stop loss that you set per share.

For long term trading to become profitable, you must be disciplined enough to stop your losses and let the profits run. Always use stop loss and take profit orders if you wish to maximise profits and minimise losses.

Stop loss orders are great protection against huge losses, in the event that the market moves against you. This is why stop loss orders must be placed in every trade. Write down your exact entry and exit point; a mental figure does not count.

Exit strategies are often more challenging than entry strategies, for the simple reason that your mentality and presence of mind shifts once you are in the game. As a rule of thumb when exiting, never exit your winners at once. Exit them in parts and stick to the trend for as long as possible. Hold your last part until the trend starts to reverse.

One lesson that experienced traders will tell you, is that when profit is on the table and if the profit is more than expected, you should take the profit there and then.

If you are not particularly disciplined, a take profit order ensures you exit the market after a predetermined profit is reached, reducing the risk of greed taking over your rationality.

In a live trade, you might have problems staying with your initial trading plan and targets. When profits run, you might be tempted to not exit the trade even when you have met your profit target.

Likewise, when your trade has reversed, you may refuse to cut losses and hope for the better. That is why these two orders could be the most useful weapons you could ever use against emotional trading (or even an untimely computer malfunction).

I cannot stress enough the importance of placing stop loss and take profit orders - they're the best life buoys to prevent you from drowning in the sea by helping you cut losses and maximise profits. They also free up your time away from the computer, giving you the luxury of other pursuits.

Last but not least, use not only a price time, but a time stop as well. If, within a certain period of time, the market still doesn't move in your desired direction, be prepared to liquidate his position.

4. Be well-informed

There are many things you can do to reduce risk, no matter which trading instrument you choose.

Take note of what and when economic and earnings data are due, instead of blindly plunging in with your eyes closed. Before the market even opens, check index futures such as S & P 500 or Dow Jones to get a feel of the general market mood before confirming your go-ahead for your plan.

Successful traders never gamble; they put probability in their favour. How? None other than by hard work, education and homework.

Be careful, though, of letting what you know hinder you from trading success. Mental conditioning, where our mind forms prior conceptions about the market, can stop us from seeing the market for what it really is.

An instance is determining when the price is overbought or oversold. Usually, technical analysis and fundamental analysis are used to predict if the market is going to reverse soon.

However, as human beings, we tend to form our own perceptions about when a stock is overbought or oversold, based on history and memory. This is certainly a risky thing to do, as no market level is truly unbreakable, or predictable, for that matter.

Hence, in your pursuit of education, be careful that what you gain is employed in a positive, not negative fashion.

5. Keep a Journal

Have you ever seen a lemming write? Exactly. They don't. Lemming traders scoff at the idea of keeping trading journals.

If you are sincere in keeping track of and helping your self-assessment, keep a trading journal. All good traders keep their trusty journal by their side. After all, trading is your business and you are the accountant.

A trading journal, useful to both beginner and experienced trader alike, can aid in actively analysing the thought processes and emotions behind each trade you made. When done correctly, a trade journal will allow you to understand how your personality shapes the way you trade, and pick out the strengths and weaknesses of your trading personality.

Note down all details, such as targets, entry and exit points, support and resistance levels, time of trade, market open and close that day and so on. Go as far as to jot down why you made that particular trade, your emotions and the lessons learnt.

A good trading journal should enable you to review both your winning and losing trades and zero in on the specific reasons behind these results, then come up with specific steps to address what you did right or wrong.

Here's a sample of a trading journal to give you an idea of how it can look. Of course, it's up to you to decide which format and style best suits you.

1st trade: Done on 20th Jan
No. of trades done to date: 8 closed & 5 open

Closed trades statistics:

5 wins & 3 loses

Highest pips won per trade = 554 pips, on my first trade.

Open trades statistics:

3 positives & 2 negatives

Reflections:

1. The signals did present itself after the course and have to wait for 2

2. When the signals to enter came, it came in an avalanche, meaning there were several opportunities that presented themselves at the same time.

3. Entered 3 trades per day after the 2nd day when opportunities presented themselves.

4. Found that there is a danger of entering too many trades at one go as the risk is concentrated and not spread out throughout different time period. When the market reverses itself most currency pairs can be affected.

5. When JPY goes up sharply, it strengthens against many other currencies, not just one pair. Need to be prepared for a short-term correction.

6. Initially I thought that a trailing stop is preferred as a way to auto exit a trade to achieve higher profit compared to a profit target and the profit target should be negated. However, this will reduce the profit in the case of strong prevailing trend.

7. So the rule of maximum 3 trades per day is a good guide to follow.

8. Setting a maximum risk of 5% makes me feel more at ease after entering the trade.

9. Got excited after the first win of 554 pips, but reality sets in as there are also losing trades despite meeting all criteria.

10. An automated method to calculate maximum range is necessary due to long time taken to work out the maximum range. There are some anxieties when it takes too long to decide on the maximum price pull back range. Did an excel macro for that.

11. Entering the trade with a buy limit or sell limit pending trade has the advantage of getting a good price as usually the price will fluctuate around the existing chart price a little.

12. Notice that when the trend presented itself it has already moved some distance away from the direction of my trade. I had the occasional problem of forgetting to set the trade volume before activating an order. I will do that first on every order setting.

Discipline is one of the key traits of winning traders. Start with staying committed to a trading journal. It's precisely because few people are willing to put in extra effort that makes the trading field profitable to only a select few.

Learn to plan the trade and trade the plan better by both keeping a trading journal and keeping yourself well-informed.

WHee, that was fun!
Could we do that again?

The Addicted Lemming

This particular lemming does not act in a herd, but that does not make him any better. (Worse, in fact.)

Often characterised by an alarming intensity of this lemming trader's trading, this creature loves and is addicted to the thrill of jumping the cliff more than anything else.

Unlike other lemming traders who trade to win, this addicted lemming is hooked on the high of trading as an activity; never mind the disastrous results.

If this chapter sounds like you or someone you know, acknowledge that trading has become a problem and seek help.

The Addicted Lemming

*The four most dangerous words in investing are
'This time it's different'.*
John Templeton,
Billionaire stock investor, businessman and philanthropist

Indeed, if you find yourself saying "this time it's different" before placing a trade, you might well be what I term an addicted lemming, or in layman terms, a 'market gambler'.

A trader pays great attention to the risk involved rather than the rewards, while a market gambler focuses on the stimulation and thrill of possibly immense wealth. Market gamblers often fall prey to the market when their inner desires overwhelm their ability to act rationally.

Trading is <u>not</u> gambling. Any time you find yourself approaching it out of instant gratification, halt.

Ready? Read on to see which of the following you may be guilty of.

Beginner Luck

Most addicted lemmings start off trading very cautiously, and enter more winning trades as a result. The problem comes when they start believing that they have beginner luck, without realising that it was the cautious approach that got them 'lucky' in the first place.

Like gamblers who may think they are blessed by Lady Luck, they start to let their defenses down. This is when the market shows its true colours, wiping their account dry.

In trading, there is no such thing as beginner luck. While Lady Luck may be shining on you in other aspects of your life, she backs away when she comes face to face with Mr. Market.

Never make the fatal mistake of disrespecting the market, for it will disrespect your trade in return, by burning a hole in your portfolio.

Cheap Thrill

Ever wondered why some traders continue to trade even after losing all their possessions to the market?

Addicted lemmings are in it not so much for money prospects, but more for the surge of adrenaline coursing through their body.

Risk management is absent in such addicted lemmings who desire the heart-pumping rush that comes from an impulsive trade. These people gamble with the market to gain the excitement lacking in their life. Their goal is thrill, not profit.

Market addiction is more likely to occur when our self-esteem, recognition and other needs are not met outside of our trading life.

Do not fall into this trap. Build healthy relationships, and engage in leisure pursuits that make you feel fulfilled. That way, you tend to trade when you see opportunity, not when you need stimulation in life.

Overtrading

If you have gambled in a casino a couple of times or more, you may have realised the longer the time you spent inside, the higher the probability you walked out a poorer man (or lady).

The reason is simple. Spending a longer time inside often means that you placed more bets. *As British politician Mark Fisher points out, the passage of time is the casino's best friend and the player's worst enemy.*

The same applies to the financial market.

Those who overtrade are bound to exit the market a loser. Winning traders take active stances in the market; the addicted lemming overtrades.

Never trade for the sake of trading. Sometimes the best trade is not making any trades. Disciplined traders never trade for the sake for trading, but addicted lemmings enter the market based on whim and fancy, which is akin to financial suicide, really.

Lack of a System

The addicted lemming does not follow a system.

Like a true gambler, he does not depend on research and rationale, but on mere chance. The addicted lemming ignores the rules designed over the years to cope with the uncertainty of the market, believing that his luck will bring him through.

Without a system, the addicted lemming loses, but instead of reflecting upon the losses, he blames it on luck, and is upset that more capital wasn't put in on winning trades.

Hot and Cold Streaks - The 3Rs

Hot streaks and cold streaks are what every avid gambler goes through, and I can assure you, the experience isn't anything like a sauna.

A addicted lemming may be on a lucky strike and win a string of trades, following which he believes this 'hot streak' will continue. He then increases his position size, hoping to make more money out of this hot streak. When the market changes position, his winnings are wiped clean.

In a bid to win back what is lost, the addicted lemming reenters the market with a vengeance, hoping to recoup his losses. He loses, naturally, and starts feeling like he is on a 'cold streak'. The addicted lemming feels lousy about himself, and start trading smaller sizes, but it is too late. The psychological and monetary damage has been done.

The 3Rs of Trading

I call this the 3Rs of trading. Everyone is guilty of it, at some point in time or other - even the experienced traders.

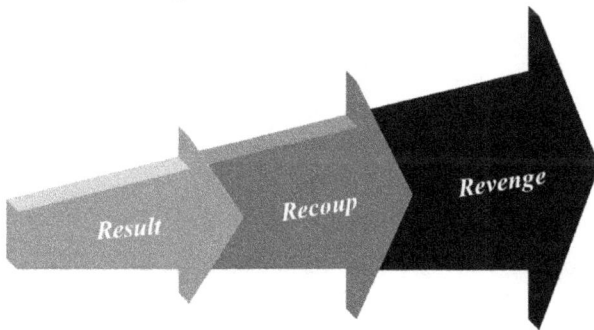

A trader starts off, focusing on the *Result* rather than the process of trading. Naturally, he trades with his emotions, is easily distracted, and ends up veering away from his plan.

He loses as a result. This time, he enters into the second stage - *Recoup*. To recover his losses, he increases his capital without regard for the market conditions.

To recoup the 5% of capital from a previous losing trade, he puts in 10% for the next round. When he loses once more, he is even more bent on recouping his losses for the previous 2 trades and puts in 30% of his capital. He is oblivious to the fact that by going against the market trend, it is akin to financial suicide.

Not surprisingly, he loses, and goes into the last stage - *Revenge* mood. Typically, revenge trading occurs before he can realise it. An irrational show hand is usually the result, and his portfolio that has been painstakingly built up over time falls prey to the 3Rs.

Monitor yourself carefully; the warning bells should ring should you find yourself falling into any of the 3Rs.

When Trading becomes an Addiction

How much of an addicted lemming are you? Do you genuinely enjoy trading, or are you addicted to it? Successful traders <u>want</u> to trade, for the passion of trading. Addicted traders <u>need</u> to trade, for the thrill and excitement.

Trading provides a strong sense of stimulation for some people, and that is what leads them to psychological and sometimes even physical dependence. They are not able to stop even in the face of negative consequences as a result of the addiction.

Addiction to trading is so common, yet there is little attention paid to it, especially in trading seminars or books. This is because the aim of most commercial trading aid is to encourage more people to trade, without educating them on these risks.

There is a thin line between losing one's discipline and being addicted. An addicted gambler will find that it is all too easy to lose discipline.

It could be people around you pleading with you to stop trading, or you yourself finding that you are too preoccupied with trading to do work or have fun. If your mood fluctuates with the market rising and falling, and you are in dire financial straits due to trading, you are addicted.

The most difficult part is acknowledging it. Do not fall into self-denial. You may think you can handle your own trading impulses, but it wouldn't have come to this if you really could. An addiction is an addiction precisely because the addicted lemming is unable to control himself without external help.

The right thing to do would be to close your account and seek help. The exchange of your addiction for your old (and probably better) life will be the best trade you ever made.

Hey, our next tip is
going to be good, really..

Leaving the Herd

If, at this stage, you find yourself thinking, 'gosh, I'm a true blue lemming trader', all is not lost!

It's perfectly ok to be a lemming trader. In fact most, if not all successful traders were previously lemming traders. The difference between a trader that makes it and one that doesn't is that the most successful (and wealthy) traders realise their lemming behaviour and mindset fast. They change.

The mere realisation that you want to make this shift away from continuing as a lemming trader is a great start.

So you're all ready to part from the lemming herd. The question is, how?

The upcoming chapters will enlighten you on how becoming a winning trader in your own league.

First, let's take a break away from lemming traders and look at how winning traders do it in the *9 Traits of Winning Traders*. Study these traits carefully, as if your life (and money) depended on it.

The second section *Golden Rules of Money Management* is just as, if not more important to ensure you keep the money you've won and reduce your losing trades.

9 Traits of Successful Traders

Sometimes, the best trade is no trade.
Old baseball saying

You may have heard that 90 percent of all traders go broke. Before you exclaim that the market is out to cheat our money and throw in the towel, realise that trading does not actually possess a track record any worse than many respectable professions.

Think about this: how many people start out playing soccer with the dream of becoming a professional footballer, and actually make it to worldwide top teams? The percentage is probably even less than that of successful traders!

Just like all professionals, traders have to dedicate a lot of effort to achieve high levels of success. There is no shortcut.

The shockingly low percentage of traders who eventually make it can be attributed to lemming traders with little or no experience throwing their money onto the market and expecting their trades to run.

Rather than focus on this ninety percent of lemming traders, let's think about why the other ten percent succeed. Although winning traders may be very different in terms of background and character, research has shown them to share many common traits.

To be successful in trading, we need to invest in ourselves to develop and emulate the following 9 traits.

1. Discipline

Discipline is one of the top qualities that you will find in any successful trader. Without discipline, even the brightest trader with the best trading plan can fail. On the other hand, a person with average intelligence can perform well in the market with adherence to a sensible plan.

Most traders simply focus all their energies on finding The Strategy that works best. But every time they don't make money from it, they assume it to be the fault of the strategy, and move on to another one. Never do they look inward to realise it is their own lack of discipline that caused the failure.

Top traders follow a plan, and stay closely to the system they have chosen. Keeping to a proven trading strategy protects them from emotional trading. These traders are aware that in a system where success rate is dependent on probability, mistakes can greatly affect profits gained on 'average'.

A lack of discipline is contagious. Rather than procrastinators, surround yourself with people who display self-control. You can recognise people with high self-discipline through their everyday lives - do they live by their New Year resolutions, or keep to a strict exercise regime?

People with discipline fight procrastination with diligence and determination. They are also less likely to be impulsive, and can control any 'destructive' behaviour once they recognise it.

People with a low level of discipline, on the other hand, tend to be less conscientious, do not plan well, and are impulsive.

There has always been this question: Is discipline the cause for trading problems, or is it a result of a trading problem?

To find out which is the case for yourself, think about whether a lack of discipline is lacking in other aspects of your life, such as relationships and your spending habits. If it is, then discipline is possibly the cause for several of the trading problems you may be facing.

Some traders may have difficulties staying disciplined in the face of increased perception of risk. When they have invested more than their usual fare, emotions may wreak havoc on an otherwise disciplined character. This is why trades should always be 'boring' - that is not to cause you alarm or panic should the trade not go your way.

Luckily, no matter whether discipline is a cause or effect of trading difficulties, individuals with low self-control and high impulsivity can always overcome their lack of discipline by following very structured, rigid trading rules closely, and mentally reinforcing the need to see them through.

What to do

Start by keeping to the little promises you make to yourself - be it attending a language class or going to the gym. With time, you'll find that you've much better control of your life, and that your trading style is gradually shifting from being emotional to theoretical.

After all, only you can instill discipline in yourself, which will in turn give you confidence from within to make your money work for you.

Here are some tips that will help you:

- Forgive yourself: Every human makes mistakes. If you harp on your error whenever you feel you're losing discipline, it may become a self-fulfilling prophecy whereby you fall into a spiral of self-blame and procrastination.
- *Simplify*: You lack discipline in doing something because it is not that easy a task to perform. Make it easier for yourself. Rather than trying to research for hours on end before placing a trade, research for twenty minutes. It is more important that you make this a habit that is regularly performed, a ritual that will be easily naturalised later on.
- *Enjoy*: Perhaps you find it hard to stay disciplined because you dislike a particular activity. Incorporate something enjoyable

into it. Tell yourself that should you stay disciplined for a week straight, reward yourself. Or do your research and planning at a lovely café playing your favourite music.

What else to do
Identify the reputable trading programs available in your area and enroll in one with a very strict disciplinary mentor who will instill discipline and impart the right trading values and psychology to you, from the start.

2. Consistency

Consistency is one of the hardest things to achieve in trading profits. Perhaps due to the freedom and degree of independence that trading offers, it is all too easy to let a lack of discipline hinder us from achieving consistent profits.

Consistency in trading is defined by Nazy Massoud, Wall Street insider and author, as the 5Cs - Clarity, Commitment, Calmness, Confidence and Courage.

Clarity
How clearly do you see and measure yourself regarding your focus on trading? Think about why you want to trade and the facts - your trading methodology and system, trading vehicle, hours of trading, the news sources and charts you refer to, and what you are doing to manage both internal (emotions) and external (trading activity) events.

The clearer you are on all the above mentioned, the more likely that your trading profits will be consistent.

Commitment

Commitment reflects the priority ranking on what is most important to you in your life. If you are not determined to make trading amongst your top five priorities, consistent results will not come by as easy.

What are you willing to give up in pursuit of improved trading performance? Are you willing to put in hard work and effort, even when things do not appear to be going your way? Or rather, go out of your way to make time and energy to enhance the way you trade? Understand your own boundaries before setting realistic targets for your self-improvement.

Calmness

Few people can start out as a trader and make consistent profits, as they are unable to forgo their emotional involvement when they win or lose. Emotions are their worst enemies. When they win, they get elated and start trading recklessly, believing themselves to be invincible. When they lose, they get demoralised and depressed, leading them to enter illogical trades.

When the market moves against you, stay calm. Instead of getting upset and moving into defensive, take a deep breath and reevaluate the situation. By staying calm, it is much more likely that your assessment of the market and your actions are wise and unclouded by emotion.

Confidence

There is a fine line between arrogance and confidence. There are some traders who insist they are right even when they are losing money. Such traders will always be consistent in their trading - in losing!

However, do not also fall into the category of traders who know what to do but never do it anyway, because they believe somehow that they might be wrong. Of course, there is always a possibility that you will be wrong. Good trading is about making consistent profits, not winning every time.

The top traders are consistent in long-term profit because they recognise that losses are unavoidable in trading. They strive for greater wins than losses instead of trying to beat the market. A casino makes consistent profits even though the dealers do not win every single bet.

Rather than procrastinate and hold back for fear of losing, take action when you feel the time is right; it's half the battle won. It's no guarantee that you will definitely win, but not taking action guarantees you will not win.

Courage

Courage is never about a lack of fear; rather, it is about going ahead despite recognising fear. Deciding when to enter and exit trades is one of the most important functions of a trader. This is why decisiveness is crucial to making successful trades.

Courage, when combined with the right amount of confidence, will push a trader to decisively make the right trading moves even when the world seems against it. How do you know when a trading move is right? This is where clarity comes in.

When in doubt, access how much your trading move is based upon research and sensibility. If you are clear on why your mind is telling you to play this trade, let your heart have the courage to follow the signals.

What to do

Consistency is one of the hardest and most challenging to any trader. By combining the 5Cs sensibly with a healthy mind, you will grow to be unfazed by the unavoidable proportion of losing trades and achieve truly consistent trading success.

If you're really serious about working hard to stay consistent, keep a journal. Use a systematic process to access your trading record and style, then evaluate the good and bad moves for each week. In no time, you'll find your trading has improved.

3. Emotional Resilience

A successful trader is never driven by fear or greed.

Instead, he possesses high mind control, is detached and treats trading as an intellectual pursuit, beyond merely a money-making instrument.

Emotionally resilient traders perform well under stressful conditions and remain calm no matter which way the market moves. They see losses as lessons to be learnt, for future trading opportunities. While even top traders may feel lousy after a particularly bad trade, they rebound quickly and become stronger; some traders never recover.

Allow yourself to learn from experience. When researchers measured the heart rate and blood pressure of traders, it was found that more experienced traders remained more stable in the face of unexpected market movements or information.

Resilient traders are flexible in their thinking, and recognise that market conditions are always changing. Rather than insist on the genius of their trading plan and take misjudgment personally, they are able to withdraw quickly instead of trying to wait out the loss.

With emotional resilience in the face of market turbulence, a successful trader is unlikely to chase market fluctuations, or give up in the event of losses.

What to do

Trade what you see not what you think. Stay calm by telling yourself that you have a plan you will stay with, and follow time-tested and proven systems. Do not be hard on yourself; always view losses as experiences. Remember, adverse events allow us a conscious choice to be a victim or victor.

It is also important that you do not trade with money you cannot afford to lose. Having to worry about mortgages or loans is often so worrying and stressful that it distracts the best trader from making rational and wise decisions.

Stop riding on an emotional rollercoaster. Take control of your feelings and emotional responses to market fluctuations, and you'll find that you can remain calm even in the most chaotic market.

4. Patience

The successful trader understands that sometimes, the best trade is no trade. He is patient and waits out the best opportunities, forgoing the less favourable ones. There are days that he goes without a single trade.

Beginners, instead, tend to lack self-control and overtrade, mistakenly believing that more trades equal more profit. For some traders, their total commission and slippage costs are more than their total profits for the year!

Patience is actually a form of discipline, and is most difficult to manage, especially during low volume trading periods. Most traders end up entering a cycle of overtrading during these periods, where there is insufficient follow-through to compensate the bad entry.

Capturing the right moves requires patience and timing. Taking trades that are not part of your trading system is known as making up a trade. If a trader does not possess the patience to wait out a good trade, he is likely to rush to find any position, inevitably leading to losses. Never get into trades just because you are bored and wish to look for something to trade.

Let's compare patient trading to fishing. There are countless fishes in the lake, and it is impossible to capture every single one. Simply focus on the few good catches and your net will be full. Opportunities are everywhere; the trick is finding those that fit your trading style and system.

It also takes patience to stay with a singular trading style and instrument you are most comfortable in. However, it is not advisable that you try out various styles and instruments; rather, focus all your energy on one or a few trading vehicles and systems and become truly proficient in them.

Patience is not only crucial during the entry and waiting period, but also while holding and during the exit as well. Sometimes, you may have followed all the rules of the system, but still ended up entering trades where the prices are not moving much.

At this point, instead of rushing to sell it off, perform a re-evaluation. If your rationale for entering the trade no longer holds given the new market situation, then sell it, but if your re-evaluation suggests that your choice was wise, be patient enough to wait out your intended position.

Only trade a small percentage of your capital each time. When many traders start making profitable trades, they start to wonder if they should raise their stakes to make bigger profits. Others wonder if they should be making more trades each time.

My advice is always to 'be patient'. I have seen many a trader become overly excited by the prospects of increased capital and trade frequency, only to be burnt later.

The reason is simple. When more is at stake, you tend to become more emotional and rash, causing you to be less desirable decisions. When you focus your attention to more trades than you can handle at any one time, you become distracted and stressed, which in turn affects your cognitive thinking.

Capital size should only be increased as your portfolio grows; that way, 3% of your capital increases exponentially as you improve on your trading, giving you the time and experience you need to handle larger amounts each time.

What to do
Being patient does not mean that you should not do anything at all. There are many things you can do to help your next trade when it comes along. Read forums, books on trading, interact with other traders, and most importantly, prepare for your trade with thorough research.

If you are an impatient person by nature, consider enrolling in trading academies that will provide you with comprehensives check lists, and only trade when everything in your checklist is met. Find a mentor you can relate to, and whom you can approach to discuss any personal concerns you may have.

5. Long-term Perspective

The good traders see their current trade as only a small part of a larger, long-term picture. Because of this macro perspective, they are able to persevere and keep going despite the losses they may face for the time being.

Successful traders never take losses personally, as they are independent thinkers with healthy self-esteem. Rather, losses are part and parcel of the trading game to them. They possess perseverance and patience to tide out the losses, in the faith that their long-term plan is right.

On the other hand, short-sighted traders may react negatively to losses, and overtrade in an attempt to recuperate lost capital from the previous losses. What often results is a downward spiral and vicious cycle that sees their portfolio health suffer.

What to do
Always remember that you can have many losing trades and still profit in the long run. Do not be disheartened or attempt to take revenge on the market, for Mr. Market will always win.

Rather, learn to focus on risk management, and always ensure that your trades offer good risk-reward ratios. Your best bet is a tried and tested trading system that will give you the confidence to persevere even if the first few trades do not garner the expected results.

6. Self-awareness

Winning traders are often people who are highly aware; they have a higher level of consciousness regarding their physical and mental state. Additionally, self-aware individuals are driven by logical reasoning behind their choices and behaviour, which explains their profitable trades.

Self-awareness is also linked to emotional intelligence, which is highly related to trading, work and even relationship success. While emotional intelligence may be more inherent in some from birth, self-awareness in trading can be easily trained with determination and a trading journal. I cannot stress the importance of reflection enough.

All traders should periodically review and access their own performance and portfolio health. By performance I mean not just the results, but also before, during the process, and after a trade. How prepared are you for your trading session? Are you updated on the latest market trends and news? Do you stick with your plan or free yourself of all reins once you log in? Do you place improvement or results as your priority?

Answering these questions may be the key to maintaining the right mindset and presence of mind needed for successful trading. When you are self-aware, you will also be more conscious of how objective (or subjective) you have been about a trade.

Self-aware traders can sense when they have shifted their focus from the trading process to the end result, and can quickly bring their rationality and focus back on track.

What to do
Keep a journal, and reflect on previous trades immediately and then again, a day after. Try to identify what went wrong or right, keeping in mind your emotional state during your trading process.

Take note also of your objectivity in a trade. Can you tell when the potential monetary returns are clouding your rational ability?

7. Accountability

Anyone who claims to never have had a losing trade is either lying, or has never traded in the first place. Rather than spend energy and effort trying to disguise mistakes, a successful trader accepts responsibility for his trading results. This means he is open to learning lessons from the market. He takes losses in his stride, and is able to get over them.

And because he does not take it personally, he manages to focus his energies into managing money and limiting losses, instead of justifying why the trade was not profitable.

It is all too tempting for us to shift the blame for our losses to a third party - the news, insider tips, or your friend's advice. But if you refuse to accept responsibility for your losses and choose to shift the blame, you're merely denying yourself the opportunity to fine tune your trading strategy and improve yourself.

Truly successful traders not only accept their shortcomings and improve on them, they also review and access their trading performance from time to time, even when they are doing well. Not only do they correct wrongs, they remind themselves to stay in the right frame of mind.

True winners know that while being wrong is acceptable, staying wrong isn't. They check on their own educational progress, knowledge of the changing markets, and their portfolio health periodically.

What to do
Never blame any third party for your trading results, or harp on the mistakes. Instead, channel all your anger and frustrations to reflection based on your journal. Not only will you improve your trading acumen, you'll also become a happier person.

8. Acceptance of random events with low illusion of control

Winning traders are fully aware that they do not have control over market price action, and accept the role of chance events in shaping market prices. They know it is impossible to control the market and that losses happen even with the best strategies. There is no such thing as winning without losing.

On the contrary, losing traders feel that they have some control or sway over price movements, and do not believe in the influence of chance events on their trading performance. Because of this, losing traders are more emotionally affected by failing trades, mistakenly believing that they could have "done more". This is why some traders have more difficulty recovering emotionally from losses.

These same traders are also more likely to believe that winning trades are a reflection of their genius or proficiency. Their emotions move with the turbulent market, and rationality goes out the window.

This is the little difference that enables winning traders to cut their losses short and let profits run, while the majority does the opposite. Winning traders are able to pay attention to the process rather than the outcome, because they have minimal stress to perform, knowing that anything could happen in the market that is not within their control.

What to do
Always bear in mind that the market is a great force that cannot be contended with, only utilised to your advantage when the time is right. Never think that you can shape the market forces; perform sufficient research before entering any trade.

9. The Constant Desire to Improve

Any business requires you to continually learn in order to be profitable. One common trait of successful traders is that they value continuing education, and believe that keeping up to date with what's happening pays off.

Because of this mindset, they try to completely understand their market, and it appears much, much friendlier to them than to the clueless dude on the streets. When successful traders lose, they take it upon themselves to figure out what went wrong. There is a competitive streak in them to constantly improve themselves.

On the contrary, most traders perceive trading as the way to an easy life. Once they realise (though a few losses) that trading actually requires much hard work, they lose interest and give up. Think carefully about how much hard work you are willing to put in.

Trading is about investing not just your money, but mostly, your time. This was probably what was meant when someone said "time is money". The time you spend on educating and upgrading yourself (be it on trading or other life skills) will go a long way in helping your bank account grow.

The best traders read voraciously, from security analysis to Plato to learning about the planets in our universe. Most great ideas sprung out of making seemingly irrelevant links from cross-disciplines.

Even if you cannot devote extensive time to read widely, it makes sense to learn as much about your area of trading as possible. If you are trading telecommunication stocks, read and update yourself on the latest news and happenings regarding telecommunications and the possible factors affecting   this   business.

You can become well-versed in an industry by going to related seminars and conferences, reading journals, and analysing charts. The world is constantly changing, and no knowledge holds true forever. To stay relevant, we have to grow together with the times. The reward comes naturally later.

Winning traders continually search for new opportunities and strategies. They track their personal performance, and set extremely specific goals for each trade they place. They also progress by experimenting with new areas slowly, but backed by reason and research. An example is setting stop losses at new places. In that way, you quickly grow invaluable experience and emotional resilience.

What to do
Be not afraid of growing slowly; be afraid only of standing still. Build your portfolio slowly. Develop a willingness to invest in education, not just specific to the market, but also your personal life and line of work. Take up quality courses to start you on the right track, and read related books. The cost of such resources will more than pay back for themselves, when you see your trading skills improve.

> *To be a winning trader, emulate these proven traits of winning traders. It takes 30 days to form a good habit, and only 3 days to lose it, so be persistent. (Likewise, it takes only 3 minutes to ruin 30 days of profit!)*

Golden Rules of Money Management

Money management is like sex. Everyone does it one way or another, but not many like to talk about it and some do it better than others.
Gibbons Burke, Editor & Executive Producer of MarketHistory.com

Unlike sex, money management does not get the great attention it deserves. In the trading world, money management is regarded as uncool and not hip, as opposed to the latest trading strategies and 'hot tips' (which you should probably never listen to!)

The money management we're talking about here does not refer to saving for a rainy day or your piggy bank, but rather, how a trader should optimise his capital usage and keep portfolio health in mind.

Say we compare money management to body building. You can't possibly work out and lift weights every single day without eventually burning yourself out or sustaining some injuries that'll set you back. Rather, weight training requires a carefully thought and executed plan to optimise your training without compromising on your health.

Money management is about finding that optimum point that works for your portfolio and financial health. The key thing about money management is that no string of losses will be able to eliminate you from the trading game.

Preserving capital is of utmost importance. Without any capital, nothing can be achieved no matter how great a trader is. This is why we should never gamble and risk too much money in one trade hoping to get immense profit.

Always understand the risk and rewards for each trade. If you cannot take that risk, walk away.

The importance of good money management cannot be stressed enough. Follow the money management rules below, and you're on your way to good trading habits that'll earn you consistent profits.

1. Do not Reverse the 3 Goals of Money Management

The *3 Goals of Money Management* that I'm going to share is probably the closest thing to the 'magic formula' of trading, if there's such a thing in the first place.

Survival → Profit → Exceptional Profit

This is the way that millionaire traders play the market: they first aim to not lose (survive), then to more winning trades (profit), before proceeding to increased capital when their portfolio growth increases (exceptional profit).

Lemming traders and beginners tend to reverse these 3 goals. They first aim for exceptional profit by putting in large amounts of capital, once they enjoy a few consecutive wins. They then start to lose, and hope to take back some profits or just break even. Eventually, without a proper trading plan, they are barely surviving as they try to hold on to their initial capital.

Exceptional Profit → Profit → Survival

Warren Buffet puts it like this: rule number 1 of investing is never lose money. Rule number two is to never forget rule number 1.

In short, play not to win - play to not lose.

Instead of focusing on making money, focus on protecting what you have. Learn to take losses, and learn to control the downside. Good traders practise defensive money management - they take care of the downside, and never worry the upside. *All traders make mistakes; great traders, however, limit the damage.*

Forget winning - the most fundamental rule to making money in the market is survival; to not let your losses get out of hand.

For instance, never add to a losing position - it's accelerating your plunge downwards; it's suicide. Sounds like common sense, but all lemming traders have this problem. Fueled by hope, they ignore their stop loss and put in more capital, believing that they were right about the market trend, and that if they plonk in more capital and wait, they'll more than make up for the loss later. Often, they drown.

To become a winning trader, never reverse the 3 goals of money management, tempting as it may be.

2. Do not Overtrade

In trading, when there is nothing to do, the best thing to do is nothing.

Easy enough, but not easy to follow. Lemming traders find it hard to not trade when his fellow mates are happily trading away. Not surprisingly, overtrading is one of the most common reasons for a lemming trader's demise.

Never trade for the sake of trading.

It's important to know when not to trade. Do not overtrade. You know you're overtrading when you:

- trade outside your trading plan
- trade beyond what you are capable of understanding
- trade to make up for previous losses
- trade a significant percentage of your portfolio

Additional tip: If you have 3 trades in a row wrong, stop trading for 1 day, as this amplifies that chances of you becoming prone to recoup or revenge trading.

If you have 3 trades in a row right, stop trading for 1 day, as greed may get the better of you.

3. Trading is a Marathon, not a Short Sprint

Forget 'get rich quick' - go for 'get rich slow' instead. Wall Street stock investor and research consultant Peter Lynch points out that stocks are a safe bet, but only if you stay invested long enough to ride out the corrections.

Trading is a marathon. The hare and tortoise story our mothers told us couldn't have been any truer. In trading, the tortoises win, and get rich as well.

Understand that trading runs in cycles. There will always be good and bad days; hang in there. *Never let a down period demoralise or immobilise you, and don't measure your results short-term.*

Traders who believe in getting rich quick are those who fall victim to 'hot streaks'. A lemming trader may enjoy a string of several winning trades and, believing in getting rich quick, start feeling confident of his hot streak. Instead of recalculating the percentage of trading capital and keeping to the initial percentage as per his trading plan, he increases his capital dramatically to take advantage of the 'winning' streak.

Unfortunately, when the position goes against him, he has lost all his profit from prior winning trades.

Always keep the larger picture in mind. Never get carried away by wins or losses. So long as you keep to a logical trading plan, the losses will be balanced out by greater wins.

4. Always Keep Your Trade within 0.5% to 5% of Your Capital

The essence of risk management is deciding how much to buy or sell. If you buy or sell too much, you increase the risk of losing beyond what you expect. Take too little risk, and your reward is too minimal to cover the overhead of your efforts or even the transaction costs.

The best risk taker manages to locate the right spot between these two extremes.

Whenever a price trend is established, one would add to the position and move the stop tighter because he knows that trending only happened a few times. This is contrary to common folks who exited prematurely.

\Many trading strategies teach you when to enter and exit a market. I go one step further and advocate risk management. Imagine you have $10,000 in your portfolio, and decide to risk $2000 each trade. It'll just take five consecutive losing trades, and you're out of the game!

Risk should always be incremental.

Think of it like soccer: a penalty shot taken at the start of a match, versus a penalty shot towards the end to determine the winning team. It requires the same techniques and skills, but you can imagine the immense psychological barrier amplified ten times over in the second scenario.

Reduce this psychological pressure by keeping your risk small and constant.

Remember that risk management is a thermostat - a control system to keeps your trading within your personal comfort zone. Only increase your trading size gradually, for traders who enter impulsive trades often find themselves psychologically unprepared, like our soccer player here.

Larry Hite, the forefather of system trading, advises to never risk more than 1% of your total equity in any one trade. This allows him to be indifferent to any individual trade, and hence stay rationally calm in the knowledge that he is not losing more than he can afford.

In my trading course, I advocate keeping your trade within 0.5 to 5% of your portfolio, depending on your comfort zone, initial capital size, and individual risk profile. This way, you'll find that your emotions are less likely to get the better of you, and you will be much better able to make rational decisions.

Always practise defensive risk control.

Experienced traders control risk, inexperienced traders chase gains. While entrepreneurship may be celebrated where you come from, conservative traders always have the last laugh.

About The Authors

Choo Koon Lip is the founder of Forex Asia Academy, a leading Forex Practitioner Hub serving the Asia Pacific region. He believes that as one becomes consistently profitable in the forex market, he will also find himself becoming an enlightened individual with a higher level of self-awareness. A self-confessed movie buff, a good movie makes Koon Lip's day anytime.

Joey Gu is an advertising creative director who marvels at the beauty of an industry that celebrates a dynamic integration of creativity into business. Joey enjoys doodling and coming up with sticky marketing ideas that leave an impression. Lavender tea is to her what catnip is to cats.

You don't need to know who you are in the market;
the market will tell you.

www.ingramcontent.com/pod-product-compliance
Lightning Source LLC
Chambersburg PA
CBHW032011190326
41520CB00007B/425